Frog

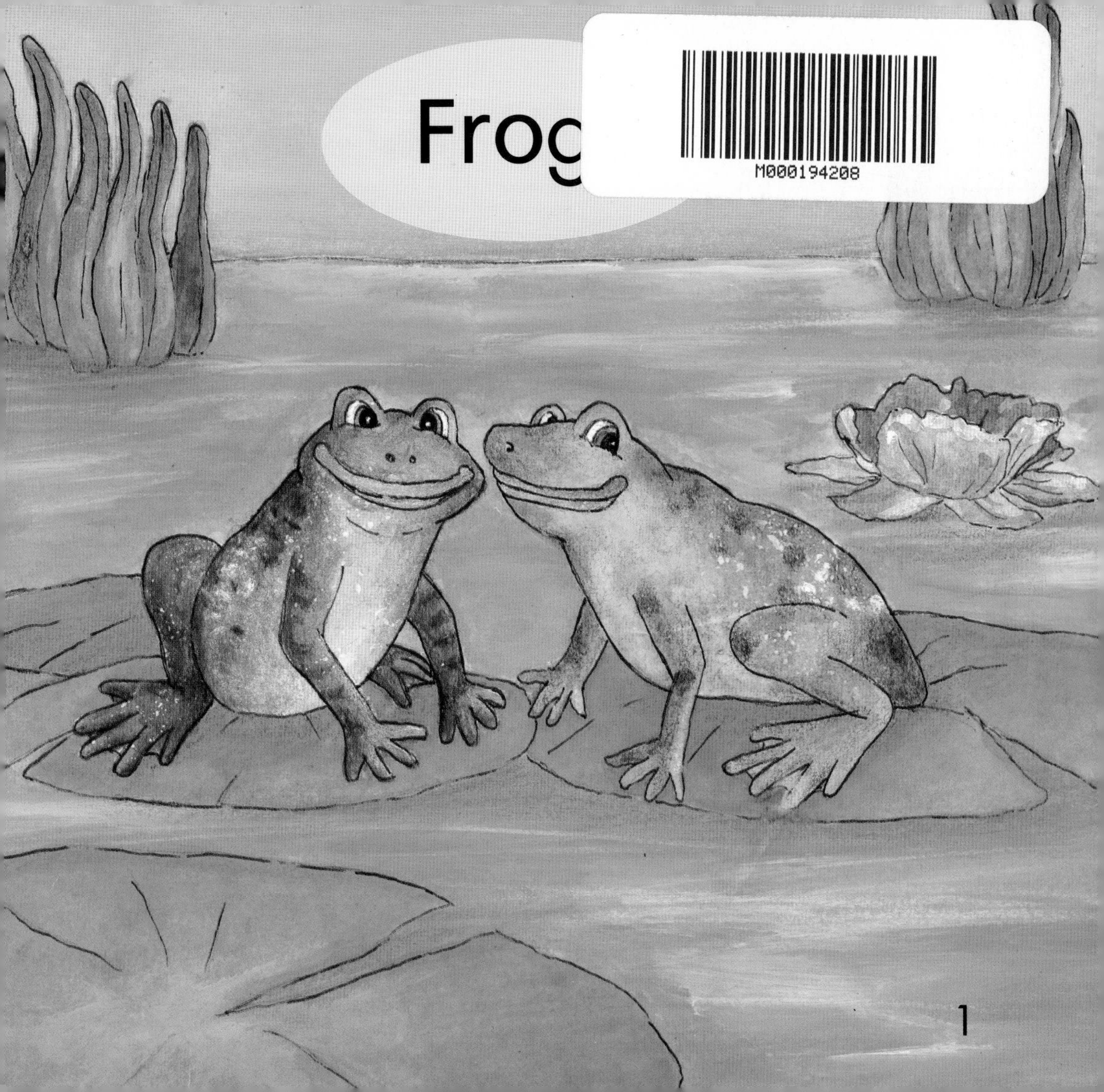

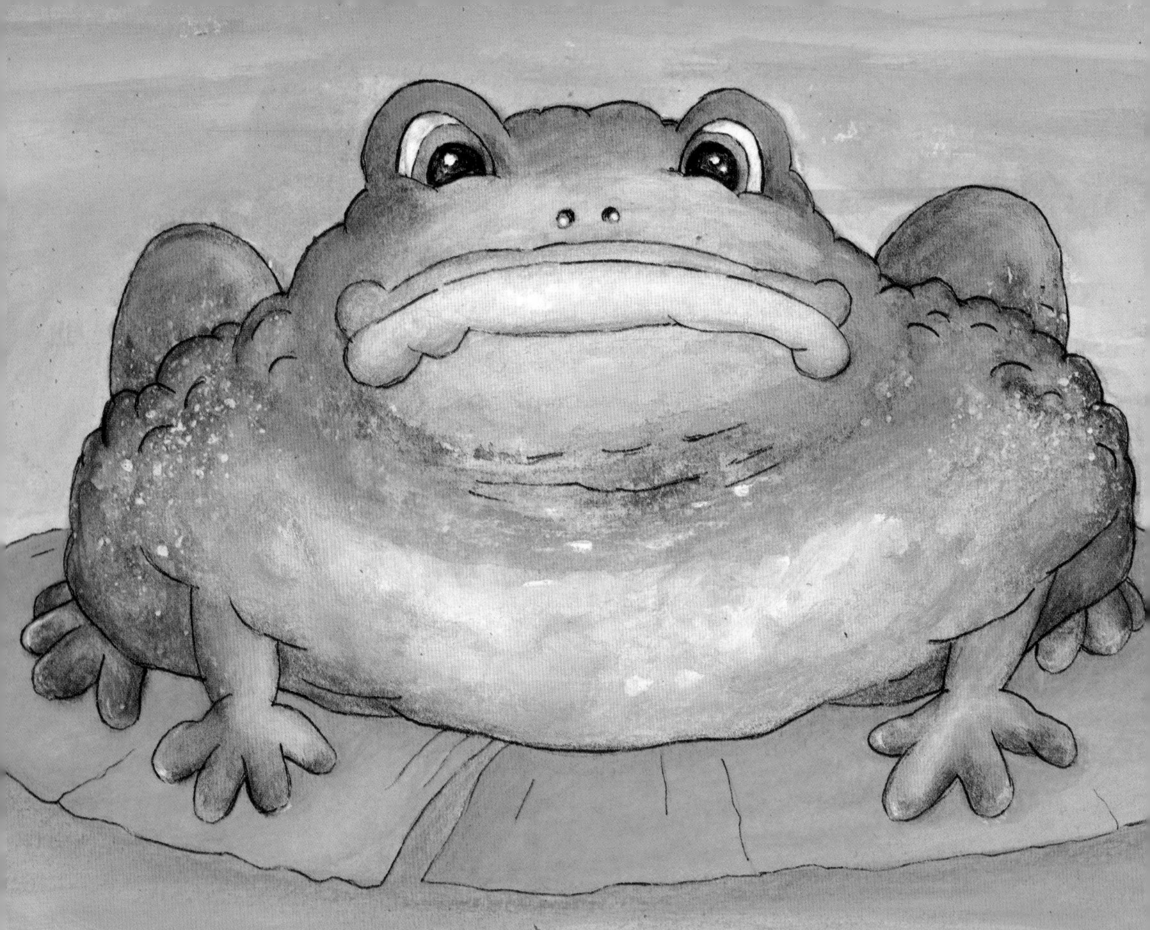

“I am a big frog.”

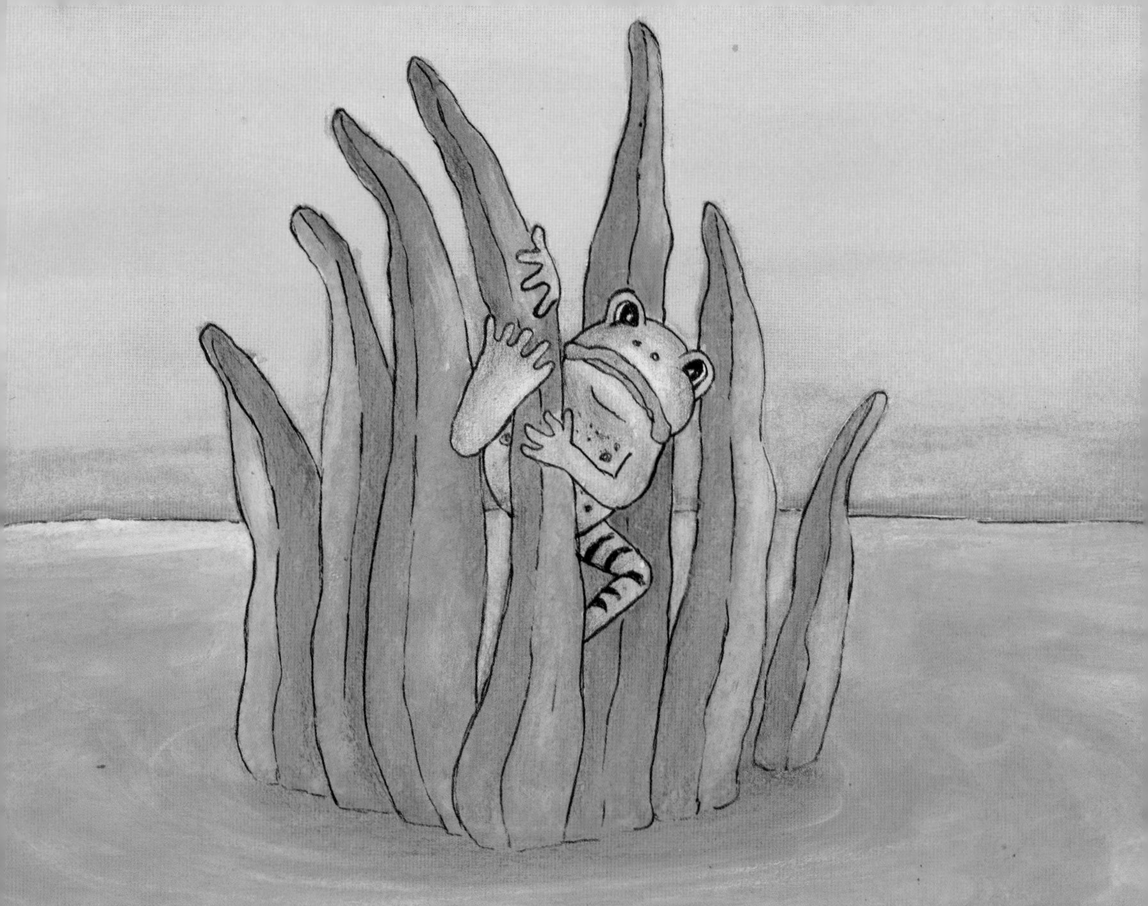

“I am a little frog.”

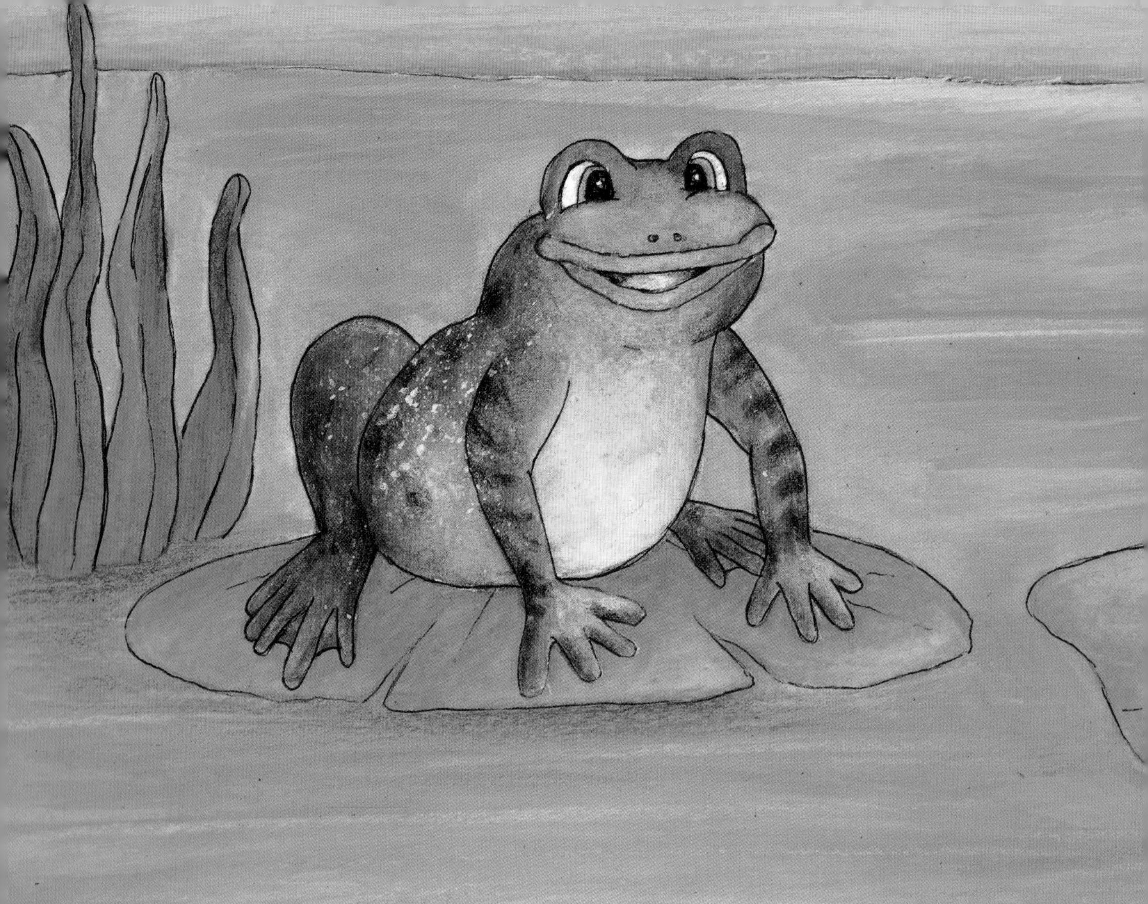

"I am a brown frog."

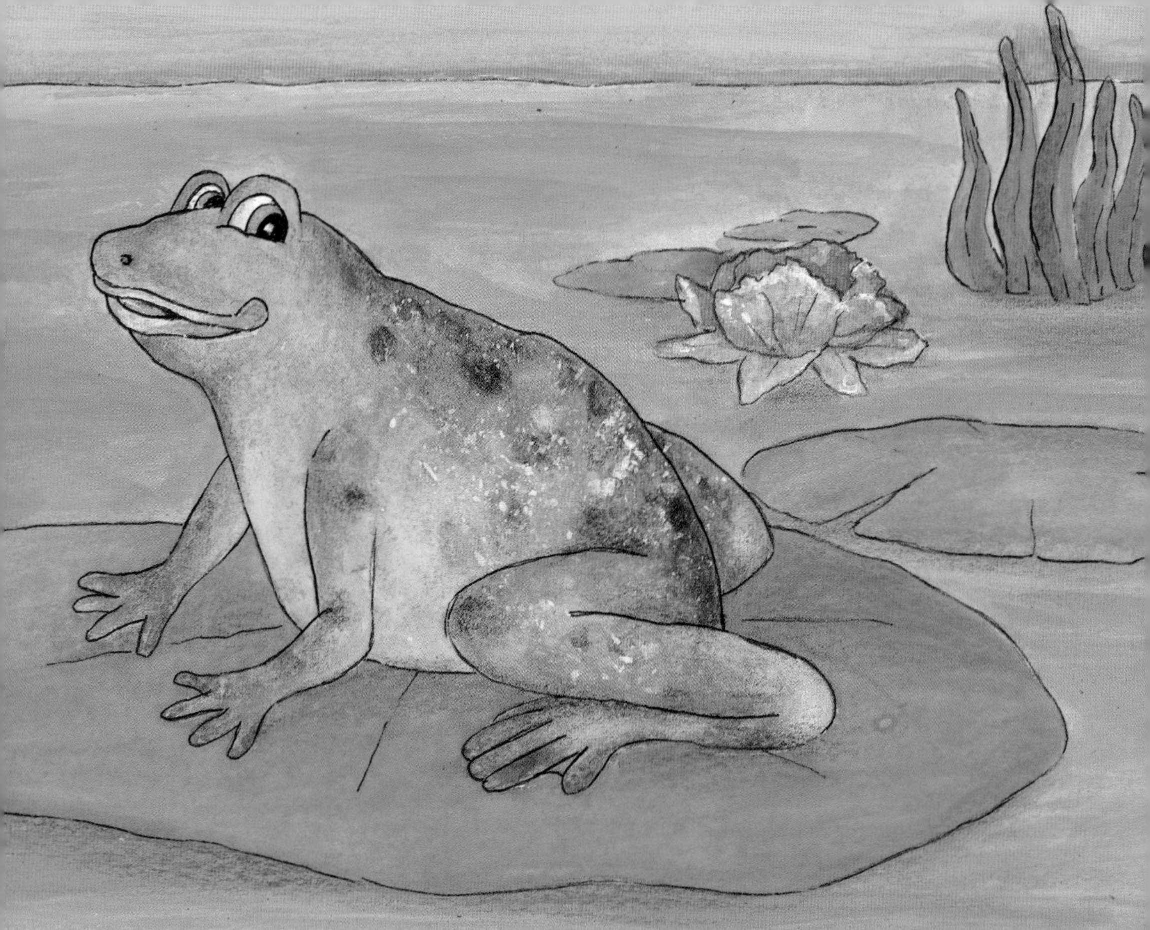

"I am a green frog."

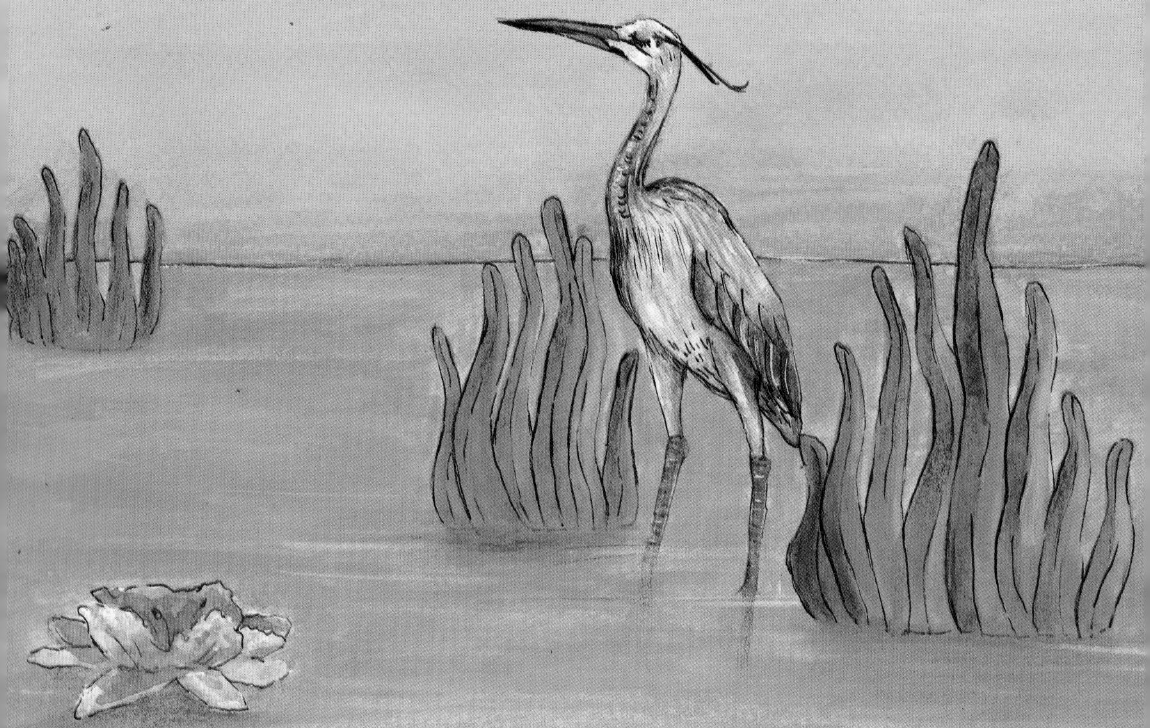

"I am a heron.
I eat frogs."

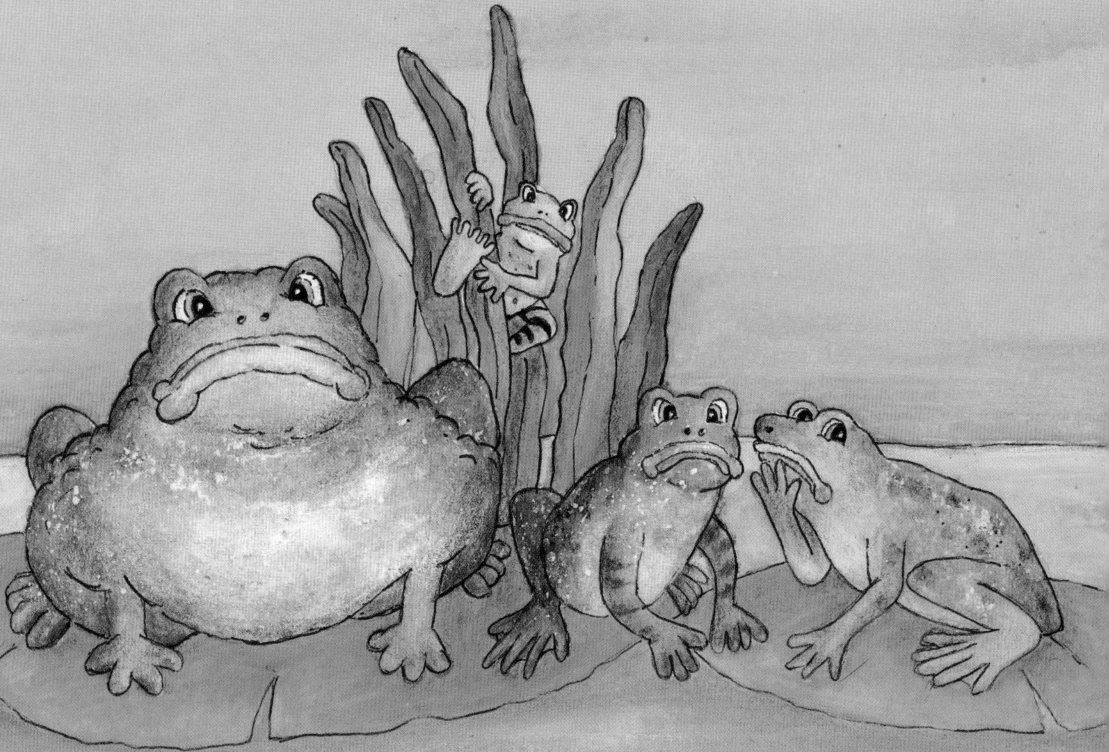

“A heron?”

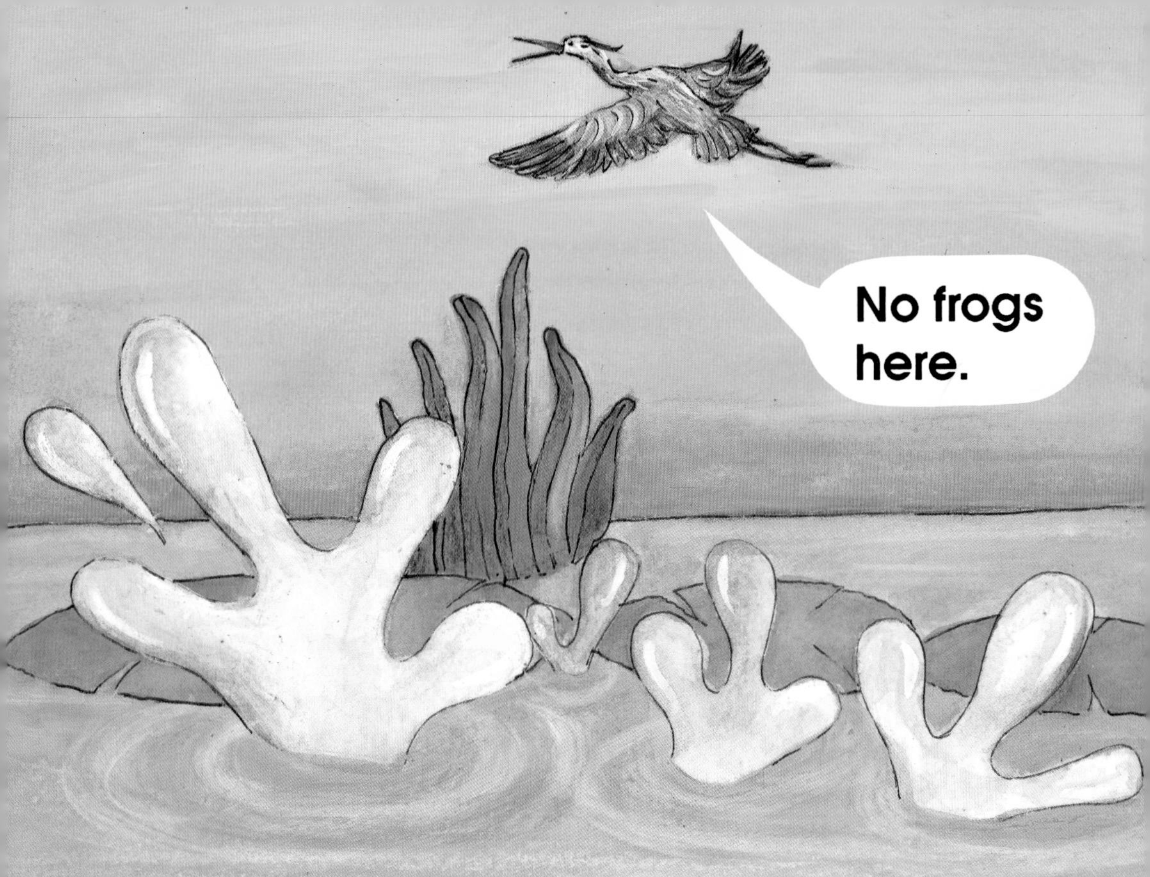

Splash! Splash!
Splash! Splash!